MW00818038

Gata
Գաթա

A Book of Shapes
Երկրաչափական Պատկերների Գիրք

by: Hrachouhi Zakaryan

For my nephew William
Սիրով՝ իմ քրոջորդի Վիլյամին

The illustrations in this book were made using gouache on illustration board.

Text and Illustration Copyright © 2022 by Hrachouhi Zakaryan

All rights reserved. No part of this book may be used or reproduced in any manner whatsoever without prior written permission from the publisher.

First edition 2022

Zakaryan, Hrachouhi

Gata: A Book of Shapes.
Գաթա. Երկրաչափական Պատկերների Գիրք:

Summary: A bilingual book in English and Armenian that teaches children about shapes and introduces them to Armenian themes and culture.

Printed in the U.S.A.

ISBN- 978-1-7350579-2-7

Circle

Círcle

Square

Քառակուսի

Triangle

Եռանկյունի

Rectangle

Ուղղանկյուն

Oval

Ձվաձև

Trapezoid

Սեղան

Diamond

Ադամանդաձև

Heart

Heart

Star

Աստղ

Semicircle

Կիսաշրջան

About the author

Hrachouhi Zakaryan was born in Armenia and grew up in the United States. She earned her BFA in Illustration from the California State University of Long Beach. Zakaryan strives to make art that inspires people to connect with nature and the Divine.
She lives with her husband Artavazd and daughters' Arevik and Lilit in Southern California.

Գրողի մասին

Հրաչուհի Զաքարյանը ծնվել է Հայաստանում և մեծացել Միայցալ Նահանգներում: Նա իր նկարազարդման բարձրագույն կրթությունը ստացել է Կալիֆորնիայի Նահանգի Լոնգ Բիչի համալսարանում: Զաքարյանը ծգտում է ստեղծել այնպիսի արվեստ, որը մարդկանց ոգեշնչում է կապնել բնության և Աստվածայինի հետ: Նա ապրում է իր ամուսնու` Արտավագդի և դուստրերի` Արևիկի և Լիլիթի հետ հարավային Կալիֆորնիայում

If you would like to purchase a copy of this book or any other art please visit:
www.etsy.com/shop/hrachouhi
or email hrachouhi87@yahoo.com

Made in the USA
Las Vegas, NV
11 December 2024

13889573R00017